Clocktower Books

Sator Enigma:
❧ Ancient Roman Mystery Solved At Last ❧

by
John T. Cullen

2000 Year Old Riddle Deciphered and Explained

Clocktower Books, San Diego CA 92120 USA

Contents

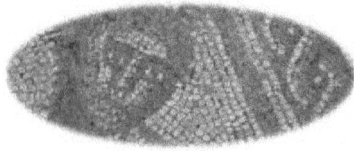

Author's Preface to the 2021 Edition

The ancient Roman Sator Square (also: Rotas Square) is an enigma that has baffled scholars for centuries. I can now offer the definitive answer to what the Sator Square really meant across the ancient Roman world.

My finding reinforces our saying that truth is stranger (and more powerful) than fiction.

I can assure you: it has nothing to do with the occult, or with aliens, or any other half-baked conspiracy theory. It is not a spell, nor a charm, nor a curse formula. And it does mean something. Its ancient but timeless wisdom offers a very powerful guide for our daily lives today.

The Sator Square is telling us a very down-to-earth, amazingly pragmatic, powerful aphorism (saying). Its truth reflects not only Roman small-town farm society from before imperial times, back over 2,000 years ago to the Roman Republic. Beyond republic and later empire, the Sator aphorism or saying later also reflects the fundamental underpinnings of neo-Classical and European Medieval philosophy and theology right into our own day and age.

I will reveal the solution in the next few pages. I'll need the rest of this book to explain the context of those five simple words, which are:

SATOR AREPO TENET OPERA ROTAS

Here is just one of many examplars. This one is inscribed in stone, and found in Cirencester, U.K. (courtesy Cotswolds District Council). The British-Roman city was then known as Corinium.

The fact that we find the Sator Square to have been displayed publicly and prominently across the ancient Roman world tells us it was a key and universal emblem.

The inscription is found across the ruins of the ancient Roman empire, often in key government or military locations, as well as public squares (*fora*) like that in Pompeii. Another example has been found in the ruins of a key military headquarters, the doomed major Roman fortress of Dura Europos on the Parthian frontier.

Exemplars of the inscription are found scratched, carved, or painted on walls and other surfaces in locations from Cirencester, England to the public exercise square in Pompeii to the headquarters of Dura (Fort) Europos in Mesopotamia.

We can now, at last, understand the answer. Those five words may have evaporated along with the Latin *vulgus* or vulgate (common language spoken across the empire), but their meaning and their spirit live on in the foundations of modern civilization. I will prove my assertion in this book.

Until the end of Late Classical Antiquity around 500 C.E. (A.D.), the Roman empire was a vast nation without internal borders. According to modern estimates, the empire contained roughly fifty to seventy million souls or more across much of Europe, northern Africa, and western Asia—an area today divided into more than one hundred nations of many cultures and languages, many of them frequently hostile to each other.

The Roman nation shaped itself upon a powerful cultural, political, religious, economic, and military foundation. The complex daily processes of that nation were a great engine that powered them to keep their vast domains together (albeit with much internal strife and no small number of external threats) for about half a millennium. The Roman colossus began breaking up after a significant defeat by the Goths at Adrianople in 378 C.E. and the sack of Rome itself in 410 C.E. by Germanic barbarians (Christianized Goths and their Germanic allies). Scholars refer to various dates that signal when the empire in the West died, including 476 (when the last emperor at Rome, a teenage usurper named Romulus Augustulus, was sent into exile). My own preference is 537, when the Goths destroyed the aqueducts bringing millions of gallons of water a day to Rome, and the city quickly deteriorated into the European Medieval village it was to long be, with maybe 25,000 or so villagers left to huddle in their huts on the Tiber, amid apocalyptic ruins all around; forests containing lost temples and streets and palaces.

In that state of affairs, let's say safely no later than about 550 at most, much of the common culture of that formerly great nation was lost. Included in that loss was any understanding of what the Sator Square might have meant.

Our concern in this book is about five important little words. A small but important part of the loss, as the eastern Roman empire (Byzantine) went its own way, and the western Roman empire broke up into Germanic (Gothic,

Vandal, Suebic, and their like) kingdoms, was the popular meaning of this mysterious inscription we today call the Sator Square. It is also known (for reasons I will explain) as the Rotas Square or the Sator Rebus.

This remarkable artifact forms one of the most perfect palindromes ever known. Derived from the Hellenic (Greek) language, 'palindrome' describes any inscription that reads the same way backwards as forwards.

For example, the word 'madam' is simple example (one word, that reads the same way left to right as right to left. The playful sentence "Madam I'm Adam" is often cited as an example of a palindrome.

The Sator Square goes much farther, in that its five words can be read as a four-way palindrome (up-down, down-up, left-right, right-left) always with the same order.

Again, there is nothing occult or weird about the Sator Square. It's a powerful, down to earth, pragmatic aphorism or instruction for personal responsibility. It worked for the archaic Roman farmer in Latium where it originated, and it grew in scope with the empire over half a millennium.

Now it's time. I'll tell you exactly what it means. Bear in mind, this is a new, unique, (and I think final) translation of the Sator aphorism. As I'll explain among many other things, it is not one sentence but two, linked into an ironic expression about fate and personal responsibility. Here it is:

GOD HOLDS THE PLOUGH, BUT
YOU TURN THE FURROWS.

That is the correct, proper, and only translation of the Sator Square in its true ancient meaning. In Latin, it means the same thing whether you read it top to bottom, left to right, right to left, or bottom to top (starting with Rotas instead of Sator). It may well be the most perfect (seeming) palindrome in history. But as I'll show, the perfection is a bit of an illusion. We'll get to that shortly.

It will take me this entire book to tell you how I came up with that, but let me quickly give you a modern equivalent so you'll understand how relevant and eternal its meaning is to your life and to modern life in general.

I'll plug in a popular U.S. brand of automobiles here to illustrate.

FORD BUILDS THE CAR, BUT
THE STEERING WHEEL IS IN YOUR HANDS.

Every time you take the wheel of your car (regardless of make or model) and drive away from home, you take not only your life into your hands, but everyone else's that you meet along the road. That applies especially to drunk or otherwise impaired driving (think of the wonderful campaign for sober driving by MADD, Mothers Against Drunk Driving).

That same principle of personal responsibility applies to everything we do in life. It's a profound statement of personal responsibility, as meaningful today as it was thousands of years ago. It is relevant in every area of life including faith, salvation, civic duties; and in getting home in one piece without destroying lives and property along the way (like running over mailboxes or whatever).

There is much more to follow in this book, but let's take it just one step higher. In its ironic formulation, the aphorism teaches us about two kinds of fate that govern our lives: Sator Fate, and Rotas Fate.

The first of these (Sator Fate or God Fate) is out of your hands. If you are walking down the street, and a piano falls on you from the nth floor of a building, there is no way you could have known or changed what was about to happen to you.

On the other hand, Rotas Fate governs all those areas for which you have personal responsibility. The aphorism was found on the walls of military headquarters, and as a long ago U.S. Army enlisted soldier, I can readily imagine it on the wall of one of my former headquarters. In the Army, we were taught all sorts of canned phrases of that sort.

But the meaning of the Sator Square goes far beyond

that into realms like augury and civic religion. I'll cover all of that for you in this book. In particular, it seems to echo the fundaments of neo-Platonism, a Classic philosophical system that had a powerful impact on European Medieval Christendom in terms of doctrines like sin, salvation, and free will. It's all there.

* * * *

Among other things, we'll see in this book why the Sator Square has proven so deceptive and baffling to post-Roman eyes. I don't believe that the palindromic inscription was its initial form. Based on the universality and instant sense of its wisdom, we can be sure that it was a powerful proverb of the pragmatic ancient Roman farmers long before some clever soul fashioned it into its final format.

When the western Roman empire faded away in late Classical Antiquity, to be replaced by a mosaic of cultures including much of Medieval Europe, Latin gave way to less inflected languages that do not enjoy the same sort of gymnastic freedom as a language in which expressions (e.g.) "Marcus hit the ball" and "The ball hit Marcus" may mean the same thing in Latin, but have wildly different meanings in modern, less highly inflected languages that build upon sentence order rather than declined or conjugated word endings.

Very importantly also, the ancient Sator Rebus gives an illusion of perfect symmetry that is simply not there. This is another factor that has misled translators for centuries. Then also we have the illusion of perfect symmetry that is simply non-existent. The rebus is not one sentence, but two sentences of unequal length, standing in powerful ironic opposition to one another.

Let's jump in and learn all the delightful details…

Please Note: more info and updates at
www.satorarepotenet.com.

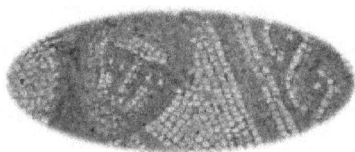

1: Ancient Secret

With bestselling suspense novels like Dan Brown's *The Da Vinci Code* and *Angels & Demons*, a trend emerged in recent years toward fast-paced thrillers about someone who deciphers an important ancient code. The heroes and heroines of such stories suddenly find themselves on the run for their lives, chased by all sorts of gun-wielding heavies. Typically, the Vatican, the U.S. Government, and other convenient players throw shadowy and dangerous agents into the mix. In the end, after harrowing adventures, the world is saved for the moment, and the hero and heroine get a brief reprieve while the next installment signals itself at the ending.

I was amused to think, while attending a 2009 convention of the International Thriller Writers in New York City (of which I am an Active Member; and Clocktower Books a recognized publisher), that I must be the only one among hundreds of thriller writers in that hotel to actually have deciphered a major ancient code. Lucky for me, so far no gun-wielding thugs are chasing me, and the world seems safe from the Sator Square (also known as the Sator Rebus, or the Rotas Square).

This article is a personal account of how I had the great fortune to spot something nobody else has apparently ever seen, and developed the first-ever plausible translation and explanation of this ancient mystery.

What a cipher it is! For centuries, scholars have been

trying to understand the enigmatic code of the Sator Square, without significant result. Hundreds of papers have been published by top scholars in various disciplines, from History to Linguistics, from Epigraphy to Classics. At least one person completed his Ph.D. thesis at Yale University on the Sator Square. Famous writers like C. W. Ceram and Jerome Carcopino have weighed in over the past century or more. Dr. Rose Mary Sheldon, Ph.D., Chair of History at Virginia Military Institute, has compiled a bibliography of all major work done for the past century or more, which was published by a cryptology journal at the U. S. Military Academy, West Point. The Sator Rebus is one of history's most tantalizing mysteries, many centuries old--perhaps the world's oldest mystery cipher at that, whose meaning was lost toward the end of Late Classical Antiquity as the Latin vulgate evolved into less inflected languages, and key assumptions of ancient imperial life were lost.

The Sator Square has proven to be a baffling, world class mystery that will not go away and will not rest.

Was it important? Without revealing a clue about its meaning, it has seemed obvious to scholars that a cryptic inscription found prominently displayed across the entire Roman Empire over a period of centuries must have had some profound meaning. But what universal meaning did it have to the generals, soldiers, senators, emperors, bishops, and governors of the world's first quasi-global empire?

Some recent scholarship tentatively points to a military connection, since some exemplars of this ancient mystery have been found inscribed on the walls of military headquarters from Britain to Syria. As I will explain, there is a military connection—but that is a subset of the larger implications of this rebus.

As with all historical problems, it is amazing how much we know and, at the same time, frustrating how much has been lost. Within months of my discovery, I was privileged to visit a secure facility at Yale University. Curators wheeled out an exemplar taken from a wall of the ancient Roman fortress Dura Europos, whose ruins lie in today's Syria.

In this article I will reveal the world's first plausible explanation of the Sator Square, and its profound meaning in human history.

* * * *

Why the cover image? The cover image of this article shows a twin-headed wall fresco decorating a wall in the Villa of the Mysteries in Pompeii. There is no direct connection with the Sator Square (whose five enigmatic words I have written under the image), but the image suggests the mystical depths of Roman culture as do quite a number of mythological frescoes surviving in ancient Roman ruins. The gaze of awe and faith mirrors the general theme of the wall paintings of that house, and suggests the same sort of profound spirituality as the Sator Square. The art work in that villa has also not been completely deciphered, since it points to one of the mystery religions whose rituals and tenets were kept strictly secret. The whole point was that you had to be an adept to get into the cult in the first place.

I have separately authored a short article about ancient Roman numenism (see Bibliography: The God Page), the animist religious foundation of their belief systems that helped the Romans to rise to a historical greatness that, when historians read or investigate, they most often come away in awe, speaking of 'the Roman achievement.' As I will point out in other articles, the rediscovery of Classical times and themes has been a regular theme and marvel of more modern cultures ever since the last Roman governors and civil servants and their families after circa 400 A.D. or C.E. abandoned the far-flung regions of the empire and returned to the homeland (from Africa, from the Baltic Sea, from the Scottish border, from the Red Sea, and more.

As an aside: Other meanings of the twin heads have been suggested. My initial, compelling guess was that the two heads, in this minor fresco, represent the two personifications of Persephone, daughter of the grain goddess Demeter. In a myth dating as far back as the New Stone Age, and current throughout the Mediterranean for millennia, Persephone is the virginal daughter of Demeter. Persephone is abducted into the underworld by Hades, who ravishes her and keeps her prisoner. In protest, all the gods and goddesses turn to Zeus for justice because the seasons have gone awry, nothing is growing properly, and the world is in disorder. Finally, a compromise is worked out. Persephone gets to spend half the year (spring and summer; see the life-like face with the green leaves) above the earth, and half the year underground (fall and winter; see the paler, ghostly face) as a shade or spirit. It is one of the threads of Neolithic legend. I actually suspect humans were already harvesting as Mesolithic hunter-gatherers, but weren't fully in a regular annual planting-waiting-harvesting-celebrating seasonal mode yet until the Neolithic Revolution (and Epipaleolithic in the Fertile Crescent) not long after the last glaciation ended. As happened in actual life many thousands of years ago, in early Neolithic cultures a related thread in the mythos tells us about kingship: the king is ritually executed as an atonement for his people's sins, goes down to the underworld, and is reborn triumphant. Sound familiar? Oh, and the two halves of the Neolithic miracle are (a) rebirth and (b) fermentation, as in beer or wine. *Hmm...* those themes survive in many modern religious observances and rituals, just as the Sator Square never loses its freshness and meaning.

Was the Sator Square part of an ancient mystery religion? Or was it a Christian artifact? As recently as 1923, the Sator Square coughed up another of its tantalizing secrets, creating even greater mystery, when it was alleged that its letters can be rearranged to spell the words *Pater Noster*, leaving *A* and *O*, possibly Alpha and Omega, as in *I am the beginning and the end*. But let us not be too hasty to fall into pat and ready, well-worn grooves and clichés. The Sator Arepo 'Our Father' is not likely a reference to the Judeo-Christian God, but (far earlier) to Roman Jupiter, "Father of Men and Gods," as cited in Virgil's *Aeneid*.

Jupiter (Deus Pater) in turn is a manifestation of the Hellenic and Hellenistic Zeus or Zeos of primordial pedigree (*Theos*, God; PIE *dyaus*, etc.) who is father of men and gods in his own right. And there is the Father of whom Jesus repeatedly spoke...could that entail a Hellenistic influence, given the battle within Judaean culture between the pro-Hellenistic Sadducees and the anti-Hellenistic Pharisees (who also went after Jesus on many occasions, according to Christian scriptures).

Welcome to our very own house of mysteries...

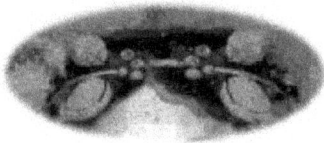

In the summer of 2007, during years of research for a nonfiction guide to ancient Roman topology, I chanced upon an old curio: the Sator Square. I had been aware of its existence for decades but, like most readers, was pushed away by the cryptic and opaque nature of its five words. I had no idea that I would one day solve the mystery (as I can now modestly but confidently state).

Those five words seem to make no earthly sense, but must have been overwhelmingly important in the Classical world. I am about to explain the entire enigma.

This is perhaps the most perfect and wonderful palindrome ever created. A palindrome is a word or group of words that reads the same forwards as backwards. For example, the word *madam* is a one-word palindrome. Here is a sample palindrome:

Madam I'm Adam.

The Sator Square is far better: a four-way palindrome. You can read it the same way left to right, right to left, up to down, and down to up. Try it—take a look at the exemplar above. You'll see why it is just as often referred to as a Rotas Square as it is a Sator Square.

By the way, you'll also see it described as the Sator Rebus. What is a rebus, you ask? It is probably a European Medieval invention, in an age when a late form of popular (vulgate) Latin was a universal language of commerce, education, and church across the many languages and dialects of Europe, and it refers most commonly to a game or a puzzle. It is a form of the Latin word *res*, which had about as many applications as our modern English word 'thing.' Specifically, it is the ablative plural in the declension of *res*, so it's *rebus*, which means roughly 'about things' or 'about stuff.' It is actually the first word in the elided (one word made out of two) word pair *res publica*, best translated as 'the public business.' From that, we derive the modern English word *republic* (for which it stands, right?).

Ancient examples of the square can be found all over the Roman Empire, from Britain to today's Syria, in Africa, and certainly in Italy. In Roman Britain, exemplars found in Cirencester and Manchester are of a variety called the Rotas Square, because the order is reversed: Rotas Opera Tenet Arepo Sator. The meaning is the same.

Medieval and modern examples are found on churches across Europe, for example the Duomo in Siena.

When I came upon it in the summer of 2007, I probably uttered an initial gasp of exasperation. Even as I pushed it away, a sudden revelation floated to the surface of my thoughts. Intrigued, I decided to take a break from the research on my Rome book, to play with the Sator Square. I saw something nobody else had seen before. I realized that the Sator Square is a mystery hidden in plain sight, in the finest tradition of thrillers and suspense novels. Only this is a true story.

It took me a few weeks to sort out what I had uncovered. Once I had the initial insight, it did not take long to tease the rest of the information from plain sight into plain meaning. For me, personally, as the hidden meaning floated into view, it was like developing a photograph in the stillness of the darkroom, and being startled at the emerging clarity of what had been a muddle. Without commenting on the Shroud of Turin, just for example, I am reminded of how startled the amateur photographer Secondo Pia must have been on a May evening in 1898, when he accidentally discovered that the photo-negative plate of a photo he had taken of the shroud showed a much clearer image of the purported crucifixion victim than the actual faint, sepia image on the shroud. There is no connection between the Sator Square and this shroud, and I only mention it as a measure of my amazement when, finally, at last, the Sator Square made perfect sense in its linguistic, religious, philosophical, and historic contexts.

2. History, To Start

When the Western Roman Empire came to an end, many of its tantalizing mysteries were buried in the sands of time.

Whatever its meaning in the Classical age may have been (and I'll endeavor to reveal that in this article), in the Dark Ages the Sator Square became a plaything of mystics, a toy of alchemists, a riddle of witches and heretics as well as orthodox churchmen, a mysterious code of Christianity, and—as I will show—a cornerstone of neo-Platonic philosophy and theology.

Countless scholars have devoted significant time to studying the Sator Square, and have published many papers or books about it. Since at least 1881, there has been an incessant stream of interest from a number of academic disciplines.

The Austrian composer Anton Webern, who wrote palindromous, atonal pieces, ultimately celebrated the sublime mystery of the Sator Square in symphonic form in his *Quartet for violin, clarinet, tenor saxophone and piano, Opus 22* (1930).

He had no idea what it meant, but he sensed (as most people do) its oddly powerful if hidden message. To the ancient Romans, in Latin, it was clear as day. When Western Roman civilization faded away, so did much that was obvious in a great civilization now forever lost.

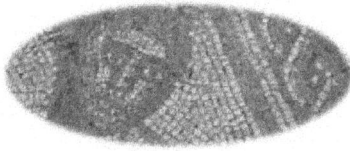

3. Words Themselves, a First Take

Sator.

Literally, *sator* means 'the seeder,' or 'the begetter.' It is also a metaphor for God--not so much the Judeo-Christian *monotheos*, but just as well the Roman father of gods and men, Jupiter (as well as the Hellenic Zeus or Theos).

In fact, just as early Christians did not use as their key symbol that emblem of shame, the cross on which the most vile of common criminals were executed, so it is quite likely that no Christian would have dirtied his or her thoughts with a powerful 'pagan' saying.

Arepo.

Nobody has ever found th word *arepo* used, in any language that could conceivably have been connected with Rome--neither Greek, Etruscan, Gaulish, nor even Proto-Indo-European (PIE), the theoretical mother language of half the modern world's languages.

Some, like Jerome Carcopino and I (separately), have thought that it is a form of an ancient Latin or Gaulish word for 'plough'. Others argue that it is a proper noun, probably a name.

One scholar was suggested that *Arepo* derives from the popular Roman-Egyptian deity Harpocrates.

Another school of thought argues that *arepo* is a nonsense word, and that the Sator Square itself has no meaning at all.

If, however, the Sator Square has no meaning, then why did the Romans transport it all over their empire over a period of centuries, and prominently display it in military headquarters, fora, and other public spaces?

In any case, the word *arepo* has proven to be the most frustrating and baffling element of the Sator mystery. I agree with Carcopino on this one. I'll explain my belief that it is a shoe-horn word for 'plough,' made to fit the five by five format of this palindrome.

We should bet that the Roman farmers' saying about the aphorism existed long before some literate person, maybe trying to be clever at a party in a seaside villa of the rich along the Tyrrhenian coast, turned it into the symmetrical, beautiful palindrome that we see amid the ruins.

Tenet.

Tenet is a verb meaning 'he, she, or it holds.' Notice
that the word tenet makes a cruciform in the center of the
palindrome. At the letter N, *tenet* intersects itself. Those
who feel the Sator Square has a Christian connection point
to that as a crucial piece of evidence. However, as I will
show in this paper, the cruciform itself has a much more
ancient usage of great importance for augury in Roman,
Greek, Etruscan, and other cultures. There were many
representations of God the Father, long before Christians
came along. For example, the name Jupiter in Latin is an
elision (joining together) of the separate words *Deus Pater*,
literally meaning God the Father.

Opera.

This word is generally taken to be a noun used as a
participle (a noun used as a description), meaning 'with
effort,' from *opera, operae* (f) effort, related to *opus, opera*
(n), work. In the sense generally assumed for the Sator
Square, the usage would be the ablative case of *opera*, the
feminine noun indicated at the start of this paragraph: again,
'with effort.'

Rotas.

This word is generally taken to be a noun form. Readers have tended to see it as meaning 'the wheels,' in the accusative plural of *rota, rotae* (f) 'wheel.'

Totally wrong. It's a verb meaning 'you turn' as in the modern English verb 'wheel' (from the noun 'wheel') whose infinitive form is 'to wheel' which is a figure of speech based on the image of a wheel turning.

Let's briefly look at a summary of the general scholarship, and then we'll crack the code.

I've already told you the solution, but we will do this systematically.

4. History, Continued

Many scholars, over centuries, have attempted to crack the Sator Code (to borrow and paraphrase a now-famous book title of U.S. author Dan Brown, *The Da Vinci Code*). The most exhaustive bibliography of their books and papers is kept by Dr. Rose Mary Sheldon*, Ph.D., Chair of History at Virginia Military Institute. Dr. Sheldon is an expert on ancient secret services, spies, and cryptography.

In 1914, a Dr. S. Seligman published an article titled *Die Satorformel* (The Sator Formulation) in a German scholarly journal. He summarized all the work done to that time. Since 1881, there have been a flood of papers on the Sator Square, all without satisfying result. Much of Seligman's finding has remained in place to recent times, except for a startling Pater Noster (Our Father) connection discovered in 1923 (which, as I have stated, does not imply any Christian connection, but strongly points toward God the Father, Jupiter).

Among the many theories listed by Dr. Sheldon are the following.

The French scholar Jerome Carcopino (1881-1970) believed *arepo* to be related to a Gaulish word for plough--which echoes my finding, except that I have found an antecedent PIE root (*ar-*) that is likely the ancestor of many words, including the Gaulish *arepennis* and the quasi-Latin *arepo*.

Other scholars have felt that *Arepo* is a proper name,

perhaps of a man or a god.

The most common reading has been: "The sower Arepo holds the wheels with effort." In my opinion, this is meaningless. No gem of insight will ever be plucked from this absurdity.

C. W. Ceram suggested the rebus be read boustrophedon style (back and forth, as the ox plows; ironic, given my plow theory), so that it would read something like "The Sower Arepo the work holds, holding the work is the sower Arepo." Again, with all due respect, this is meaningless and will forever remain a flashlight without batteries, shedding no light.

Dr. David Daube (1909-1999) of Oxford and later University of California, Berkeley, felt that *arepo* is a reference to Alpha-Omega, which occurs among other places in Revelations 1:8 of the Christian Testament. We will let that and other cups pass us by.

The Welsh poet and scholar Dr. J. Gwyn Griffiths (1911–2004) saw *arepo* as a reference to the baby Horus, or J Harap/Harpocrates, an Egyptian deity fondly adopted by Mediterranean sailors and spread to most port cities.

Some theorists have felt that the Sator Square was a Christian invention, a sort of secret handshake like the fish and Chi-Rho anagrams, used by members of the persecuted sect to communicate with one another.

I see no connection, but will remain neutral on this issue, for reasons that will become evident. Again, it is clear that Sator (Sower) is an epithet widely used by Roman authors in reference to Jupiter.

The Christian conjecture received momentum with the proposal that one can rearrange the letters to form a simple, non-palindrome construct in the form of a cross that reads paternoster left to right (but not right to left) and top to bottom (but not bottom to top)--with two letters left over, A and O, which some interpret as meaning Alpha and Omega as in the following depiction:

```
              P
              A
    A         T         O
              E
              R
PATERNOSTER
              O
    O         S         A
              T
              E
              R
```

Most scholars today feel that this is likely a pure coincidence. I am more inclined to think it is, if anything at all, a nod to Jupiter, Father of Gods and Men, or the Hellenic Zeus, whose name derives from *theos*, god.

It has been pointed out as well that the letters alpha and omega, which have taken on metaphorical significance in Christian mythos, do not perhaps exercise the same ancient warrant—since the more common Hellenic expression for doom or death lay with theta, not the last letter in the typical Hellenic alphabet, but the first letter of the word thanatos, meaning death. In short, trying to stretch the evidence to conform to a Christian paradigm is simply another manifestation of creationism, fitting the evidence to create a theory rather than the honest and logical opposite approach of allowing the evidence to lead us to an unbiased result that can be verified in the petri dish of logic.

None of these translations and theories—too many to name here, a few examples given—has provided a satisfying translation or explanation.

Let me now go back to my translation, and a brief personal history of its discovery.

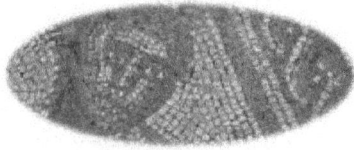

5. Insight and Translation

In the summer of 2005, as I was researching Roman topology for *A Walk in Ancient Rome* (a virtual tour of the ancient imperial capital), the Sator Square floated up in some accidental context.

When I first wrote this paper, to my knowledge, to date no exemplar of the Sator Square had yet been found in or near Rome itself. More recently, I have read of an exemplar being found in the ruins under or around a basilica dating to ancient Rome. Had there not been any, that might have set up some need for speculation. As it is, it is perfectly logical to see a find in the area of ancient Rome (which is much smaller than modern Rome). Many of the late Roman structures were built on earlier ruins dating to the pre-Christian era, so no Christian connection need be inferred. At the time of my initial interest in solving this mystery, the closest known were two exemplars from Pompeii, the city destroyed by volcanic ash and debris in 79 CE. Since Pompeii became a sort of time capsule in that year (under the Emperor Titus), we have clear proof that the palindrome in its final form was already existent. That does not necessarily mean it originated in Pompeii in the years just before 79 CE or AD.

In 2005, I did not go looking for Sator. Sator came looking for me, like a cat rubbing against my ankles and purring to be noticed.

I did notice, and it still took me at least two weeks to

understand that, contrary to all previous scholarly guesses, the Sator Square consists not of one symmetrical sentence, but two uneven or asymmetric sentences juxtaposed in ironic overall meaning.

As I looked at the words, *sator arepo tenet opera rotas*, and their usual translation into a single sentence (e.g., some form of the order *The sower Arepo holds the wheels with effort*, the word *rotas* caught my eye. That was the first of a series of game changing moments for me.

Rotas can be translated in two ways. One is the noun usually associated with the Sator Square, *the wheels*, as the direct object of the verb tenet, *holds*. That in my opinion is entirely incorrect.

What if we translate *rotas* as a verb? It translates as the present indicative, second person singular, *you turn*. Apparently, nobody has done this before, so I was walking (to borrow the expression) on untrodden snow or soil.

This opens the Sator Square to a totally new translation. If *rotas* is a verb, this means we have not one sentence but two. The first sentence has *tenet*, holds, as its predicate. The second sentence has *rotas*, turn as its predicate.

A couple of things took me several more weeks to puzzle through. What I ended up with was:

God holds the plow,
(but)
you turn the furrows.

That is the meaning of the Sator Square (or, as some sensational thriller writers might say, the Sator Code).

That is the core of my result.

A surprising amount of consequence follows from that point.

I have concluded that the Sator Square is an ancient aphorism, or motto, entirely in Latin, informed by the agricultural society of early Latium. Rome may have been (arguably) the largest city on earth before London in the 1800s, or one of the largest, but her culture was nurtured in the soil. The Roman was a farmer at heart.

The earliest known exemplar of the Sator Square, found in Pompeii, can be dated as sometime not long before the explosion of Mt. Vesuvius that destroyed Pompeii and nearby towns in 79 CE. Since the Sator Square aphorism is not found in any surviving literature, it had to be a popular construct. For several reasons, beginning with the seeder and plow motifs, it probably originated in the countryside, rather than in among the luxury resorts of the Bay of Naples. Since it is Latin, and since the area around Neapolis was part of Magna Graecia (Greater Greece, the name for the collective colonies of Classical Greek city-states in Italy and Sicily), it is likely that the Sator Square was at first a spoken aphorism further north among the farmers of Latium. They might have said: *Sator aratrum tenet, sed opera rotas*, "God holds the plow, but you turn the furrows." When this became a written artifact, cleverly shoehorned into a palindrome, the *sed* (but) was dropped, and *aratro* or *aratrum* was shoehorned to become *arepo*. I suspect that Carcopino, if he were still with us, would be delighted at this approbation of his instinct.

Let us take the individual words again, one at a time.

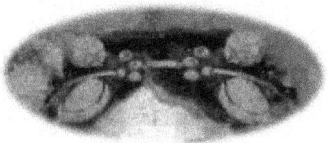

Sator

God—for the moment can be either the monotheos (one God) of Jews and Christians, or Jupiter of the polytheists.

Arepo

Arepo is a shoe-horn of *aratro*. By shoe-horn, I mean a word form that is forced into a lesser number of syllables, as we might write *lite* for *light* or *rite* for *right*. The reason for this is obvious--to fit it into the five by five format of the Sator Square. All that the creator of such a square needed was for the reader to readily understand what was meant. And that understanding would be clear from context, as I will show.

Aratro is an ablative case or possibly even a dative case declension of the noun *atratrum, -i* (n)., plow, meaning 'by means of a plow.' As we saw, Jerome Carcopino picked up on the Gaulish word *arepennis*, half-acre, which is related to plowing. But, even deeper, I have found a common root in the PIE:

$$ar \ni-$$

This stem forms the root or basis for many words related to earth, plowing, etc. in the languages derived from PIE, like Latin and Gaulish . The *e* written backward is a sort of schwa-sound. This can be found in Julius Pokorny's Indo-Germanic Dictionary*, and other PIE lexicons.

\

Note in passing that there is an obscure usage of *teneo*, mentioned in Cassell's Latin Dictionary*, whereby its object takes the dative case when used in the sense of 'holding for' or 'making for' a destination. It appears to be used with the idea of holding a tiller or sail, and in a more general sense to persevere.

The muddle is that we expect the plow to be a direct object, ending in *–um*, but that is one of the blemishes of the Sator Square, which I will address shortly.

In Latin, it was common to add a neuter suffix like *–um* or *-mentum* to a verbal (participle) as a generic 'thing of.' It's sort of the ending of last resort, when the gender of an object or condition is unclear. It's kind of like saying "that sugar thing" when referring to diabetes, as a quick example.

We do this in English with suffixes like *-ment*, *-ation*, or *-ity*. For example, the verb *arguo*, *arguere* (to explain, put in a clear light) takes the participle (a verbal that is used as a noun or adjective) *argutus*, *-a*, *-um*, depending on the gender, but the common form is *argumentum*, hence English *argument*. Similar considerations apply to many other words, like *implementum*, *imperium*, *instrumentum*, etc.

So I'm postulating that whoever invented the Sator Square as a written artifact had to shoehorn something into the second slot to not only fit the five by five format, but also to make sense in context. The closest they could come was *arepo*.

Who did this? I imagine a clever aristocrat, sipping diluted wine among his peers on a honeyed, balmy afternoon in some Pompeiian villa perhaps, steeped in Homer and Virgil, and outdoing each other in cleverness and conceits in elegant and educated conversation. I hope he (or she) won the laurel crown for best party trick that evening. But the saying itself was probably much more ancient by then, because the entire metaphor smacks of farm and soil and toil.

Here is a remarkable (stunning) bit of concordance to my theory, found in the first known instance of the Sator rebus (in Pompeii), which cannot be later than 79 CE (the eruption of Mt. Vesuvius).

An exemplar of the Sator Square in the *palaestra*, or exercise area, in downtown Pompeii, has what appears to be a stylized plow blade motif scratched directly over the *o* in *rotas*. Here is a cleaned-up version (Federica Pagliari*) of the grainy photograph of the original *sgraffito* scratched into the wall:

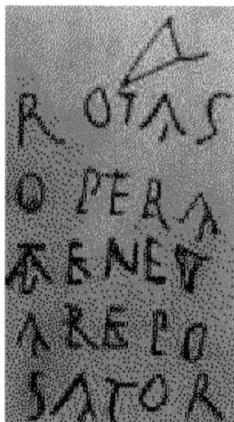

The object above the T in ROTAS is almost certainly a plow blade. The Romans employed a primitive form of cutting plow, unlike the more sophisticated Gaulish (*arepennis*) deeply cutting plow that came later. In my opinion, this startling image really tends to tighten the connection between *arepo* and plow, and the entire metaphor as I have reconstructed it.

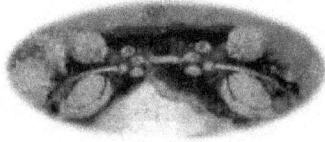

Latin, unlike English and most modern European languages, is a highly inflected language. That means a lot of information is contained in the endings of words. The ending of most nouns tells us the gender, number, and case of the noun.

Often, the ending of the noun also tells us the use in the sentence, by its case, although that has to be understood in context. With verbs, similarly, the ending tells us the person (first, second, third), number, and tense. This means that you can mix up the order of most Latin sentences, and they'll almost always continue to mean the same thing.

By contrast, in English we have to look to the context and sentence order to get the meaning. "Gerard plucks the rose" does not mean the same as "The Rose plucks Gerard" as it might, in Latin, with the correct case endings.

This loss of inflectedness is a key reason why the Sator Square's meaning became lost after the fall of the Western Roman Empire around 500, and the beginning of the Medieval period.

Tenet

Tenet is the simplest of the words. It simply means "he holds," taking an implied masculine from the *–or* ending of *sator*.

The first sentence reads *Sator arepo tenet*, or God holds the plow. The ironic thrust can be understood when we consider its antithesis in the second sentence.

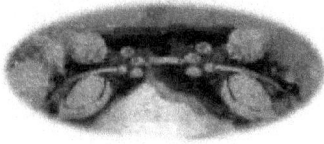

Let's look at our second sentence: *Opera rotas*, you turn the furrows.

Opera

Opera is an interesting word. First of all, it takes many meanings on the surface. It's like ordering "the works" on a pizza. *Opera* is the plural of *opus*, a work. Because the Latin people of Rome and other cities and towns in Latium were farmers, their original religion and culture were heavily agrarian.

For example, Mars was not originally a war god, but the chief agricultural god, a principal warrior against blight and drought. His name was variously Marmar, Mavors, and other variations. Roman religion is filled with agricultural and pastoral deities, from Faunus to Bacchus, from Flora to Maia.

Latin is also, like all languages, fluid across time and space. For example (one of many) consider that Ianus, the male deity associated with doorways and transitions—who became the two-faced god of January with an old face in back and a baby face in front—was originally Diana, a goddess of the moon and the hunt related to the archaic, feral girl-goddess Artemis of Homeric lore (who I suspect, by some other name, was already a female hunting deity in Stone Age times).

Bottom line: we must not assume that anything in ancient speech is fixed or permanent. Language is always a moving target. Grammarians and linguists don't sit in the locomotive, driving the train, but usually end up trying to run after the caboose to catch up with spoken language. Those of us who are bugs on grammar, usage, and style however also know that the use of common rules greatly enhances understanding and accuracy in written communications (where body language and other circumstantials cannot serve to shade the meaning).

There is, in Classical literature, a figure of speech called metonymy (Gr *meta*, change + *onoma*, name). When we use this tool of speech, we substitute an attribute of something for the thing itself.

Modern teenagers may say *wheels* instead of *car*. "I've got wheels" in this context does not mean that the person speaking has several wheels hanging around his or her neck; it means he or she proudly owns an automobile.

In the same way, *opera* (works) has been used by some Roman writers (noted in Cassell's Dictionary* among other sources) to refer to farm work. I believe that is the case in the Sator Square. *Opera* refers to farm work, but more specifically, in the context of *sator* and *arepo*, it refers to plowing.

Rotas

Rotas, if understood as a second person, singular, present indicative verb ("you turn") makes the direct object (*opera*) of this short sentence even more specific. You are turning the furrows with the plow. *Opera* refers specifically to the resulting work of the plow. The person plowing cuts rows or furrows into the earth.

An explanation is in order about *rotas*. The 'turning' does not refer to wheels (a noun or substantive). We do away with the notion of *rotas* as wheels in the context of plowing. The Romans at this point did not have the more advanced plow with wheels that helped steady it, which was actually a later Gaulish invention. The Roman plow was a much more primitive affair. It was essentially a scratch-plow, for cutting the earth.

Rotas, therefore, has two senses or subtle meanings here. The obvious meaning is that the person operating the plow must turn it at the end of the field to create the next furrow. Interestingly, the ancient Romans had long, narrow properties to minimize the need for turning cumbersome oxen (horses were not standard for plowing). The subtle meaning is that you, the plower, constantly guide the plow, while Jupiter only holds it in his figurative and moral possession.

So what does the Sator Square really mean? Why is it important enough to appear across the empire in important places like military headquarters and public squares?

S	A	T	O	R
A	R	E	P	O
T	E	N	E	T
O	P	E	R	A
R	O	T	A	S

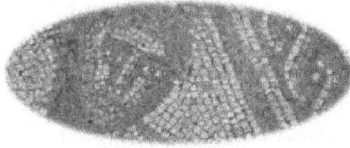

6. Fate and Sator

The Sator Square is an ironic aphorism, similar to the old Russian saying, "Cut once, but measure nine times."

A modern equivalent might be: "Ford makes the auto, but the wheel is in your hands." This would make a powerful slogan for Mothers Against Drunk Driving.

The Sator aphorism marks an important turning point along the way from animism and polytheism to philosophical and Judeo-Christian polytheism. To drive toward an understanding of Fate in its earlier context as well as the more rigorous sense of later monotheism, it is good to sketch a brief outline of spiritual evolution here.

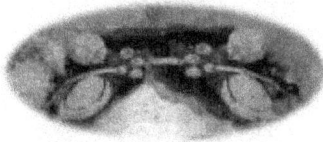

Archaic Roman religion was animistic at its core. As a relevant aside: In my article *The God Page**, I have divided history's religions into three great modalities: animism, polytheism, and monotheism. I will have much more to say on this topic in other writings to come.

Most of us understand monotheism because we were generally raised exclusively in it, and taught to abhor (and misunderstand) the other modalities. There is one God, with a capital G, who possesses all the will power or command power. He is served or opposed by mortals (ourselves) and myriad unnamed spirits who have no divine nature of their own: saints, angels, devils, the ordinary dead, etc. but most relevantly the *numina* (unnamed spirits who are silent but communicate through nods or gestures or augural signs if at all).

Monotheism became a permanent and important fixture on the world stage when emperors from Constantine (Council of Nicea, 324 CE) to Theodosius (who in 393 issued a decree outlawing all but the Nicene Christian religion) made Nicene Christianity the official and only state religion of the Roman empire.

What Nicene Christianity replaced as the official state religion was not just (more proximately) the polytheist (many gods) belief system of the late Republic and the Empire, but in fact, in the larger framework, a ritualistic state religion founded on archaic animism. We've all heard of Jupiter and the rest of *th*e named gods. In polytheism, one sees many named gods with elaborate mythologies or stories. Animism is distinguished by a number of features, which I discuss in separate articles (e.g. The God Page*). Among those features is the absence of all or most named deities, which leaves hosts of unnamed spirits in place to serve our spiritual ideations.

With those many things said, what role does the Sator Square play in all of this?

The point is that when we say "God holds the plow, but you turn the furrows," we are making a transition from animist and even polytheist religion to a new religion that embraces absolute values, salvation, and a new definition of fate.

Under animism, and to a great extent polytheism, we are dealing with spirits (mostly not named deities) who are not grounded in moral absolutes. Classical philosophy was naturally evolving toward a kind of monotheism of its own, independent of Christianity and Judaism. Classical philosophy also constantly dealt in absolutes, whether in a theory of forms, in aesthetics, or morality. Philosophy asked the tough questions that mythology avoided. The demise of an amoral, conveniently anthropomorphic Zeus (Theos) was only a matter of time.

So here's the key. Under animism, you are not seeking salvation. You are seeking survival. Capricious spirits want to kill you if you wander into their territory. They want to drown your child if he or she fetches water from the river. This is not a universe of good and evil. This is a universe like an arbitrary nightmare. You have to negotiate with all these crazy spirits who are often less rational than the average human being.

With the Sator Square, we see the emergence of a new vision of fate. God holds the plow: we can't control certain aspects of our fate, like birth and death. I can't control if a piano falls on me as I leave my apartment building. That is Sator fate.

To put a fine point on it, the ancients were not always sanguine about the interaction of gods and fate. There are many moments in Classical mythology when it appears that even the father of gods (bawdy Zeus or the more reserved Roman thunderer and lightning bolt hurler Jupiter) has no control over fate itself. Fate and Fates are in themselves mythological figures (to be discussed in another article some day). With sufficiency and imprecision, however, we can assign to God the Father, the Seeder or Begetter, a much greater knowledge of things to come (in a free will universe) than that of humans who can only control their own moral and practical decision making (Rotas fate).

I can't control falling pianos, but I can control the daily decisions that shape my life and my fate. I can choose to do the right things that keep me in the good graces of the divine, of society, and of the law. That's Rotas fate.

That understanding marks a transition from the fearful, capricious world of animism, to the moral absolutes of the monotheistic world. Of course, the drawback is, in reality, that the same human predators rule the new world as ruled the old animist world.

But that is not our most immediate moral problem or opportunity. We replace the spirit world of animism with an afterlife in which we are rewarded in accord with absolute moral principles. It is the merger of philosophy and theology. It is a triumph of logic.

And it makes sense: knowing that Sator Fate and Rotas Fate both exist, and that there is a boundary between them, takes us from a simple, rustic country aphorism to a sophisticated modern philosophical world view.

Surviving ancient times into the European Medieval and later, this concept references the Free Will doctrine of Christianity. The idea is that we cannot sin unless we have free will, which gives us the ability to choose between right and wrong. That is the Rotas choice, the part we can control by our moral decisions.

For the direct line between "God holds the plow, but you turn the furrows" to "Ford builds the car, but you hold the wheel," we have the underlying logic of the Sator Square to thank. And this thoroughly modern aphorism has further implications.

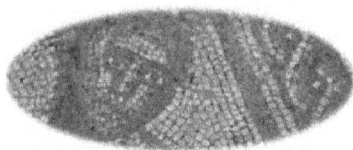

7. Augural Cruciform

The Sator Square was almost certainly originally an old oral saying of the Latin countryside. As such, it probably had some variants that have been lost. When it was put into written form, it solidified in the forms we know--the Sator Square, and the Rotas Square, which are interchangeable.

Modern monotheists, seeing the *tenet-tenet* cruciform in the middle of the Sator Square, are tempted to think that the Sator Square might be a Christian artifact. It's a notion that can neither be confirmed nor denied with absolute certainty. But one can reasonably throw cold water on such a notion. The cruciform, or cross-shape, far predates Christianity, as does god the father (pater noster).

The cross or cruciform was not a favorite Christian symbol early on. In Roman society, the cross was a mark of shame. By custom, certain types of crimes received standard punishments, in a variety of horrifying and inventive ways. Crucifixion was a particularly nasty and painful way to die, reserved for the worst criminals, slaves, and traitors. That's why the symbol of choice for early Christians was the fish, which echoed some of Christ's miracles.

Augury, reading the will of the gods, was an ancient practice already when Rome was still in the Iron Age, 1,000 BCE. As far back as we know--to ancient Sumer, at least five thousand years ago--people were practicing augury. There were many ways to read the signs of the gods. Some studied the flight of birds, or the movements of the planets. Horoscopy (study of the hour of birth, to compare with the relationships of the planets and stars at that time) is an ancient art that persists today, and its detailed studies of the heavens led to modern astronomy. Others studied the entrails and livers of sacrificed animals. The ancient Romans took augurs and chickens to war, and read the signs from heaven in whether the chickens ate or not. The very idea of numenism (based on *numina*, gestures or nods) suggests that the gods communicate with us, not in words or texts, but in gestures and signs.

The most common way to augur was to draw a cruciform on the ground, and then watch for any signs from nature. The Romans learned their initial method of augury from the Etruscans, their more advanced neighbors to the north in Tuscany. The cruciform was generally drawn in a standard manner. The Etruscans were even more precise than the Romans in many ways.

One drew a north-south axis called the *cardo*, or hinge. One drew an east-west axis perpendicular to the cardo, and intersecting it, called the *decumanus*. Quite likely, the word *decumanus* comes from a temple tax or state tax of ten percent (*decim*, ten + *humanus*, farm land, soil).

The original Etruscan method called for the observers, or augurs, to stand at the southern tip of the cross, looking north.

The left (*sinister*) was bad, while the right (*dexter*) was good. Even as the Romans conquered the Greeks, they were also absorbing the already conquered Etruscans. The Greeks introduced a slightly different method of augury, in which the observer stands at the northern end of the quadrangle, looking south. However, west, where the sun dies its daily death, contined to be associated with bad karma. The Latin word 'sinister' survives with its ill meaning intact, into modern times.

The two quadrants closer to the observer signified events happening in the near term, while the more distant quadrants signified events further in the future. The past, of course, is finished, and requires no augury.

Homer's *The Odyssey* describes an eagle flying over the sailors' right shoulders at a critical time of decision about where to head. The eagle was a totem bird related to Zeus; since that particular bird flew over the right, the eagle's presence was taken as a positive sign from the father of gods and men.

The Etruscans compiled centuries' worth of observations for comparison. The Romans relied on the Etruscans through much of the monarchy and the early republic. Wealthy Romans sent their sons to Etruscan schools to learn the *Disciplina Etrusca*, or Etruscan Method.

The Romans, and indeed most people around the ancient Mediterranean, extensively used augural methods to read the will of the gods in building public structures, all of whom tied in to the state religion.

That state religion evolved from animist beginnings, whose ritual beliefs and practices stayed embedded in polytheism and survived, in many cases, into monotheism. Purifying the altar with incense, holding processions, and lighting candles are just three of many surviving ritual practices.

To people who have only known and understood monotheism in their lifetimes, it may well seem that the Sator Square must be Christian. That is a flimsy assumption—one without merit, I think. At the same time, while Sator's origins are not Christian, the long-term effect of the Sator aphorism is stunning.

One can find neo-Platonist echoes in Christian medieval theologies forward into modern times, like vines growing around the subjects of free will, sin, and redemption. If indeed Father God holds the Plow (Sator Fate), there must still be Rotas Fate (you turn the furrows; you make daily moral decisions), and the latter affect your standing both in this life and in a hypothetical afterlife like posited for Christians and their salvation (or lack thereof due to sin induced by free will and all the other antecedents in this chain of consequence).

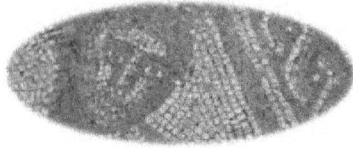

8. Christian Question

It's an issue that won't easily go away, and it has later (post-Classical) philosophical echoes.

A key question is this. If the earliest known exemplar has been found at Pompeii, is it possible that the Christians had a presence in Pompeii that early? In other words, for Christians to have possibly originated the Sator Square, they would have to have been in Pompeii before its destruction.

Jesus was crucified around 30 or 33 CE. His faith had spread at least through parts of Judea during his lifetime. We know its growth was explosive, because it offered a fresh message of individual hope and salvation for all, whose equivalent could not be found in any other religion. Classical polytheism did not offer much of an afterlife, if any. Generally, the afterworld was depicted as a gloomy, scary place of darkness and sadness (seen very graphically, for example, in Chapter VI of Virgil's *Aeneid*; and centuries earlier, when Homer's Odysseus visits the Underworld).

Many of the dead were angry for having become ghosts or shades. The idea, therefore, of an exalted afterlife for the faithful came as a revolution. It was a democratic afterlife, also, which could be achieved in equal measure by slave or emperor, man or woman, Roman or foreigner. Could it have reached Pompeii in the approximately fifty-year window between the crucifixion and the explosion of Mt. Vesuvius?

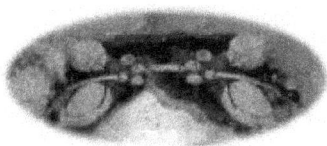

The closing theme of the Acts of the Apostles, in the Christian Testament, is the journey of St. Paul to Rome. From Acts, we learn that Christianity is first so-called at the city of Antioch, in today's Turkey, near the southern border on Syria. This happened during or just before the reign of Claudius Caesar [Acts 26-28], which would put the time frame between 41 and 54 CE. Also occurring during this time was the first council of the church, in Jerusalem, around 50. This council, which included all or most of the principal leaders of the church at that time, met to discuss issues distinguishing Jews from Gentiles within the church. Circumcision was one of the hot button topics. James said it was needed, while Paul argued that it wasn't. It seems logical to infer that the term 'Christian' then came to separate not only the Christians from the Hellenic and Roman polytheists, but the general community of both Jewish and Gentile converts from those who remained in the Jewish tradition. In the spirit of animosity that began to separate the Jerusalem church from the broadening mainstream of Christianity, Jews (perhaps traditional Jews, perhaps Jewish followers of Christ, perhaps both) accused Paul to the Roman government. They accused him of various crimes, including treason. Paul was imprisoned in Judea. He demanded trial in Rome, by his rights as a Roman citizen. Accordingly, Paul was taken in custody onto a naval vessel, which set out for Rome in 59.

The party suffered a shipwreck at Malta, where they encountered a significant Christian community. We also learn of a Christian community on Cyprus, so the faith was spreading westward on the Mediterranean. Italy is just over 1,000 miles (1,600 km) from Cyprus, a few days' sailing with good winds. In a new vessel, Paul's party reached

Sicily. They stopped at Syracuse, and then at Rhegium (Reggio Calabria, on the southern tip of Italy). They sailed past the Bay of Naples and made landfall in 60 CE at Puteoli (modern Pozzuoli). This city was famous for its fine volcanic cement (*pozzolano*) used for concrete in the Pantheon and other premier Roman structures. Puteoli was 170 miles south of Rome, and had a fine harbor for handling both grain and cement products heading to Rome.

Puteoli was roughly 12 miles (20 km) from Neapolis (Naples), and even less from the main Roman naval headquarters at Misenum. From Naples it was only a few miles to Pompeii. When Paul and his party landed at Puteoli, they were greeted [Acts 28:14] by fellow Christians, who asked the party to stay with them for a week. If there was such a strong contingent of Christians in Puteoli, surely it is likely there were Christians a few miles south in Naples and Pompeii.

It is interesting that the ship chose this city to make landfall. Puteoli was on the coastal road network leading to Rome. Whatever this naval vessel's overall mission, it apparently bypassed Naples and the supreme naval HQ at Misenum. This would put Paul closer to Rome. One possibility is that the delivery of Paul was in fact its principal mission. The Romans had already experienced generations of turmoil in Judea, which had been a tributary kingdom until the Romans felt forced to take direct charge of it as a province in 6. Gospel accounts hint of turmoil under Herod during the birth year of Jesus. In 66, just six years after the transport of Paul, Judea rose in insurrection that led to Titus' destroying Jerusalem in 70, and the siege of Masada. It seems likely that the Romans wanted to oblige Paul with a swift trial at Rome. Perhaps avoiding Neapolis (Naples) and Misenum in the Bay of Naples area was a tactical decision to avoid some popular unrest; or not. It's speculation beyond the needs of our theory about the Sator Square. Yes, there were some Christians in Pompeii; but that does not make Sator a Christian artifact.

From Puteoli, the party made their way north along the

Via Appia (Appian Road).

They were greeted in two places along the way--the Forum of Appius and The Three Taverns--by throngs of 'brethren' (presumably Christianized Jews) who had come from Rome in their eagerness. This means word had flown ahead, which suggests a rapid spread of Christianity. Paul was taken to Rome, where he met with local Jews, some of whom believed his story about Jesus, and others did not. This implies not only that there were Christians, but the doctrinal and cultural split between Jews and Christians was well underway around the empire.

For some moderns, the Puteoli story may add a shred of evidence that the Sator Square could have been either created or adopted by Christians, since Pompeii was just a few miles away near Neapolis.

On the issue of origins, however, its subject matter suggests that the Sator Square is far more likely a much older farmers' aphorism, a bit of folkloric wisdom, from the farmlands of Latium.

Also, it is utterly unlikely that a Christian artifact would be prominently posted on the wall of a major military headquarters (Dura Europos, in today's Syria) on the vital frontier with Persia.

If the Christians did not create it, it is virtually impossible that they adopted it during the imperial age. The Christians had an abhorrence for all things 'pagan,' and this would have been a prime example.

However, several twists of history conspired to make it a Christian artifact after the fall of the Western Roman empire, as we'll see shortly. First, we must explore one more tantalizing issue: whether the army contained Christians, if they helped spread Christianity, and whether they had anything to do with the Sator Square.

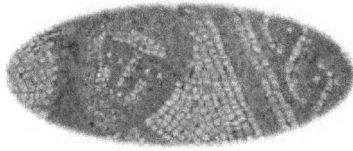

9. Military Question

Some scholars suggest that the Sator Square had a military slant. They point to the fact that many of its exemplars have been found in a military context. My own feeling is that it originated in the farm lands of Latium, as a folksy aphorism, and was eventually cobbled into the five by five palindrome with which we are familiar.

But you know what? Roman soldiers of the Republic were originally farmers recruited to fight in their archaic tribal musters. The Republic ended 31 BCE with the accession of Octavian as Augustus, ruler of a monarchy in all but name just as the late Republic is often called by historians 'an empire in all but name.' Bottom line: finding some Sator Square exemplars in military settings is no surprise.

At least one exemplar was clearly found in a military context. Dura Europos (Fortress Europos) sat astride the Euphrates River, facing the growing threat of the Persian empire. Dating to 303 BCE, the fortress was destroyed in a major Roman defeat of 256–7 CE. Among the many inscriptions found in its ruins was a Rotas Square, now kept in a secure facility at Yale University where I had the privilege to see it on a table before me in 2009.

Most young men of ancient times were either farmers or fishermen. Given an agrarian or rural origin of the Sator Square, it is certain that most soldiers of the Classical age would have readily understood its meaning.

The Sator Square might have gained special meaning in a military context. For one thing, its message is one of discipline and personal responsibility. As a non-Christian slogan, it would have looked appropriate on the walls of a military installation.

There is at least one other feature that, probably coincidentally, gives it a military slant in the Roman mind. We have already mentioned that the Romans inaugurated (used augural methods) in laying out any public building, even a city. Roman colonial cities were laid out with a *cardo* (north-south axis) crossing a *decumanus* (east-west axis).

The same can be said of the standard Roman army camp. Early in their history, the Romans learned that, when on campaign, they must pitch a complete, fortified camp every night. That prevented them from being surprised by their enemies during the night, and enabled them to pick the time and place of their fights. Every Roman army camp was laid out in exactly the same formation as any other. The *cardo* and *decumanus* echo in the *tenet-tenet* cruciform at the center of the Sator Square.

Were there Christians in the army? It seems that the ordinary Roman soldier was well aware of them, though they probably did not see them as in any way distinct from other groups and sects of Jews in Judea. We learn from Matthew 8:8-13 that a Roman centurion (military officer) came to Jesus to ask that he heal the centurion's servant. This affirms that the Roman army was well aware of Jesus' ministry before Jesus was arrested, tried, and executed in Jerusalem. The Roman empire was policed by a regular army consisting of some 28 legions, numbering about 180,000 highly trained and disciplined soldiers. There were also allied and reserve units stationed permanently around the empire. That smallish force of professionally led and well equipped regulars could be moved at lightning speed between any two points in the far-flung empire, both by naval vessels, and by over 50,000 miles of all-weather military post roads. It is likely that, in time, some of the soldiers were Christians.

Was the Sator Square a kind of secret handshake spread by Christians? It's very unlikely, given what I have presented here. Also, Christianity spread like wildfire, and needed no secret handshakes.

Many non-Christians, including the government, held Christians in contempt and suspicion before the consolidated, sole rule of Constantine (by 324, when he convened the Council of Nicea). Constantine himself did not accept baptism until shortly before his death in 337 CE. He comes across as a mediator, not to mention a flawed personality in some ways, who worked hard to keep disparate factions in line across his sprawling empire.

Despite sporadic local persecutions and conflicts around the empire, Christians were building a powerful organization as early as the so-called Apostolic Age (c33-130, the lifetimes of the apostles who had personally known Jesus). The two greatest persecutions were under Nero (65) and Diocletian (303). In-between, the Christians built a formidable organization in the shadow of the Roman empire. Constantine eyeballed the church hierarchy of bishops, priests, deacons, and lay people as the best candidate for replacing the fading traditional state religion.

During the early empire, it is likely that Christians hesitated to enlist. Being a member of the military meant venerating the emperor as a god. Gradually, Christian bishops started to define more minutely what a Christian could or could not do under various circumstances. It is possible that Christians were allowed some dispensation by the government, under some circumstances. For example, there is the legend of the Theban Legion in the 3rd Century. This legend may contain some grains of truth. A legion of Coptic Christian soldiers were brought from Egypt to Agaunum, in Gaul, in support of Emperor Maximian against the Burgundians. For some reason, perhaps because the entire legion refused to worship at a shrine to the emperor, the entire legion was put to death. If this is true, then it would seem likely they had been released from the obligation at their home posting in Thebes, Egypt, and Maximian forced the issue when they arrived in Gaul. This is fairly credible on the face of it, since Maximian was singularly responsible, along with co-emperor Diocletian, for the great persecution of 303-305, just seventeen years in the future. The Roman empire had nearly come unglued during the turbulent years from the ascension of Commodus (180) to the recovery under Aurelian (270). Traditionalists like Maximian deeply abhorred Christianity, and longed for a return to the good old days of traditional Roman religion and peace in the Golden Age of Augustus.

During the Great Persecution of 303-305, the Augustus in the West (Constantius Chlorus, father of Constantine) was not implicated, according to Christian legend. Constantine became his Caesar, or assistant emperor, in 306, and declared himself Augustus in the West in 309 (with fervent army support). According to Christian legend, Constantius had sympathy for the Christians, and may secretly even have been one himself. Adding some feeble support to this unlikely notion is the fact that Constantius' true love, Helen, the mother of Constantine, is famous as one of the most devout and active Christians of the late empire.

A final reason why it is unlikely that the Sator Square had any special Christian significance in the army is that, when Christianity became the official and only tolerated state religion, there is no sign that this in any way elevated the Sator Square's significance. If anything, the palindrome seems to have vanished—sunk under the weight of history as the Western Roman empire finally and forever dissolved.

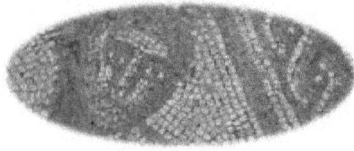

10. Lost in Translation

The Sator Square began appearing in churches, on public buildings, and as a decorative element in wealthy private homes in the European Middle Ages. Its meaning was lost, and it achieved the status of a mystical, powerful magical spell. As recently as the last century, Pennsylvania Dutch farmers, and some ranchers in South America, carved in on fence posts to ward off cattle diseases.

What caused this popular aphorism of the Classical world to become an enigma?

There are at least three major reasons.

First, it was most likely never associated with Christianity, and thus became one of the many hated 'pagan' cult properties tossed overboard during the ban on all pagan worship in a series of decrees from 381 to 393 under Theodosius I the Great. In 393, Theodosius permanently banned the Olympic Games as yet another item of cult worship. We can be quite sure that the Sator Square was one of many 'pagan' artifacts left in the dust of polytheistic antiquity. It is clear, from a sympathetic study of Julian the so-called Apostate's life, that the Christians may have wiped out Classical civilization (milestones: 410 CE, sack of Rome by a horde of Arian Christian Goths and other Germanic nations; 476, removal of last pretender Romulus Augustulus in the West; 537 siege of Rome by Visigoths, breach of aqueducts, collapse for more than a millennium of the city). But the Christians reinvented what they destroyed, from its shards and tatters over the next thousand barbarian years, with their centuries of loss and longing ultimately resulting in the twin-edged sword of Rebirth (Renaissance) which sundered Medieval understanding but created a new world order out of the lost ancient one. The Sator motif was burned with Rome, but its philosophical impact (logical, after all; rational; common sense) would not flicker out and die.

Second, the apparent perfect symmetry of the Sator Square blinds one to the fact that it is really composed, lopsidedly, of two sentences. One sentence is three words long, the other two. Further confusing is the word *arepo*, whose linguistic origin has baffled scholars for generations. That in itself suggests it is a shoe-horn, a blemish on the expected perfection of the palindrome. This is no doubt the last blush of that irrational awe and inspiration Rome still inspires, has its ghost has for many centuries; but the final realization is that the Romans were not immoral or bogeymen as centuries of sectarian lies and propaganda have insisted, but people much like ourselves who grappled (with occasional brilliance) with many of the same issues that are foundational to our civilization and therefore who we are. In other words, the ancient Roman is a guy you could sit down with and have a beer; or she is a lady with whom you could share a glass of wine and a giggle.

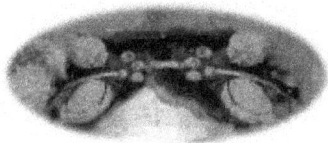

Third, a further illusion comes about with the shift from Latin to the modern Romance languages, and the resulting changes in sentence order. This is a simple, mechanical matter—so the real amazing fact is how the overturn of Classical civilization and the victory of barbarians has blinded moderns to simple facts (secrets) hidden in plain sight—like the easily decipherable meaning of the Sator Rebus when all is said and done (and we ought to wonder what the tediousness was all about, and learn from that as well).

Latin is a nearly perfectly inflected language, which means that, generally, its word endings convey much of the meaning in a sentence. Most Latin sentences can be scrambled into any configuration and still mean the same. When the Roman empire in the West broke up in the late 5th Century, the Latin of the Vulgate (popular Latin, Latin of *vulgus*, the people) broke up into dialects, which became languages.

Within three centuries, scholars say, one can detect the proto-languages that grew out of Latin, like Italian, French, Spanish, etc. Aside from Latin and Greek, the other great PIE-derived language family of western Europe is the Germanic family. This includes modern German, English, the Scandinavian languages except Finnish, and so on. A large amount of the vocabulary of these languages is Latin-derived. It's been said that English is 80% Latin. English is not a Romance language, however, because most of its key words are Germanic. The spine of English consists of mostly monosyllabic Germanic words: eat, drink, sleep, fight, go, come, fly, walk, love, hate, and so on.

All or most of these modern languages are nowhere as

inflected as Latin. English, in particular, lies at the opposite end of the scale. In a highly inflected language, you can change the word order around, and the sentence still means the same. In an uninflected language, word order is everything.

Modern people, accustomed to speaking, writing, and thinking in their uninflected languages, have been further blinded by the apparent symmetry that doesn't quite exist. Then there is that exquisite *tenet-tenet* cruciform forming the *cardo* and the *decumanus* of the Sator Square. People expect that the palindrome must consist of a single sentence, whose predicate is *tenet*, whose subject phrase preceding it is *sator arepo*, and whose direct object phrase, following the predicate in proper sentence order, is *opera rotas*.

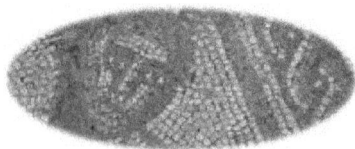

11. Conclusions

The Sator Square, as explained here, is a short aphorism, or folkloric saying, that very likely dates from the Latium farm environment of the Republic. That's before 27 BCE, when Augustus became the first of a new line of tyrants or monarchs in all but name, which we rather awkwardly call emperors. I make this observation to remind us that language is fluid, as is its meaning. Octavian much preferred the religiously based, ancestor-venerating honorific title of Augustus, in which '*au*' may have the same root as modern English awe; a feature in common with ancient terms like *augur* or *auspicium*. It is related to a visceral sense of swelling or growing, of power (as in 'augment').

The Sator rebus would have likely had its beginnings in oral form, and only became the five-word, five by five palindrome we know today when someone cleverly wrote it down sometime in the early empire.

Time will tell as more exemplars are found.

I mentioned the twisting paths by which the philosophy inherent in the Sator Square found its way into Christian theology.

Early Roman religion, a rather typical form of animism, did not deal in issues of personal salvation or moral living as a personal choice. Animism, though it has its bright side like all religions, is at heart a religion of awe, or even terror. We are terrified by unseen spirits everywhere, and there is usually no powerful father or mother deity we can turn to for help. We may inadvertently disturb some spirit by crossing a river, or hiking across a mountain, and wind up victims of that spirit's wrath.

As the aphorism of the Sator Square shows, a grass roots doctrine of self-reliance and personal responsibility grew up among the farmers of Latium, I think as early as the late Republic.

At the same time, the intellectual center of the Mediterranean shifted from Greece to Egypt after Athens fell to the Spartans in 404 BCE, followed by the rise and premature death of Alexander (c321).

In Alexandria, which had the greatest library in the ancient world, new philosophers took up the baton of Socrates, Plato, and Aristotle.

By the 3rd Century CE, Plotinus and Ammonius Saccas were hard at work, redefining what would survive in Christendom as neo-Platonism.

A whole, diverse raft of famous neo-Platonist philosophers followed, both inside and outside Christianity. Neo-Platonism is a palette of related beliefs and thoughts based on the earlier teachings of Plato.

Among them is a belief that there is some highest Good, and the idea that the universe was created by a higher intelligence than all that it contains.

These ideas were grasped upon early by Christian philosophers, who had to refute their sophisticated polytheist adversaries in debate.

These thoughts continued in the formation of Boethius, St. Augustine, and many Medieval European theologians. Neo-Platonism received a fresh invigoration during the Renaissance (1300-1500), when the church rediscovered the Greek originals of Latin documents it had been limited to for centuries.

Christendom developed a number of key ideas in its theology, including the idea of Free Will. If a person is not free to make choices, then they cannot be held responsible for either the good or the evil that they do. The idea of Free

Will makes not only sin, but also salvation possible. That concept is inherent in the aphorism that "God holds the plow, but you turn the furrows."

God, the seeder or creator, determines those aspects of our fate over which we have no control: Sator Fate. That includes our birth, and usually our death (suicide being arguably due to insanity). I cannot help it if a car hits me, or if a piano falls on me.

We, on the other hand, have control over a host of small and large daily decisions. This is Rotas Fate. We can choose right or wrong, good or evil.

A related idea developed into a cornerstone of Christian theology. Jesus said "Do unto others as you would have them do unto you, for this is the law and the prophets." [Mat 7:12].

It is not likely that a humble aphorism from the farm world of Latium in itself caused a formation in Christian theology, but it is likely that the philosophers and theologians were aware of the Sator Square and its message. It is, after all, common sense. As much as superstitious Christians probably avoided scary 'pagan' artifacts like the Sator Square, its message most likely found its way into Christian theology by way of secular philosophers, whose inquiries found their way into the eagerly waiting hands and minds of Christian thinkers.

After many centuries of darkness, a modern light shines upon this important ancient artifact. The people of long ago come to life in our minds, and we instantly recognize the profundity and the humanity of the Sator Square's message. It is a message as alive today as it was on the farms and in the army headquarters of ancient Rome. To repeat once more:

GOD HOLDS THE PLOW, BUT YOU TURN THE FURROWS.

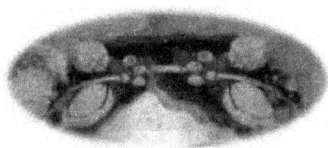

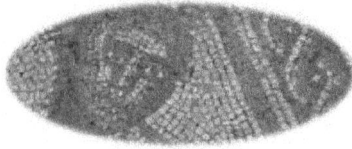

12. Postscript October 2018

As I go to press with the latest edition, it occurs to me that there is still far more metaphoric and symbolic fodder in this amazing palindrome.

I have pointed out that the word *opera* in context within the Sator Square refers to 'farm works' and would be as familiar as a world-view (an all-encompassing rule of life) to a modern farmer as it would have been in the age of the Hellenic (Greek) Hesiod (fl. 750 or 650 BCE). Hesiod, a farmer and poet, authored *Works and Days*, a poem filled with pragmatic observations on humans, society, and the farming life. It emphasizes hard work, frugality, and common sense, in addition to mythological references including the so-called Ages of Man.

Half a millennium later, around 29 BCE, the Roman poet Virgil published his poem *Georgics* (whose title refers to farm work). Like Hesiod some 500 years earlier, and Ovid shortly after his own lifetime, Virgil speaks of the same Ages of Man (Golden, Silver, Bronze, and Iron). Hesiod had mentioned an earlier, even greater age, the Heroic, which in some ways reminds me of the relative perfection of the Garden of Eden in Jewish literature.

One reason for the grouping of such ages traditionally might be that it serves king lists in one form or another: meaning that it supports a reigning monarch's claims to being descended from the divine. Sargon of Akkad did this, leaving the Sumerian tongue as his courtly language while the rest of the region became Semitic-speaking (language family of the Akkadians). That turned a long ago Sumerian king (Gilgamesh) into a divine ancestor of Sargon. Echoes of the same king list concept are found in Solomon's 'begat' list, along with other dynasty-reinforcing tropes (e.g., the flood of Noah is in many ways an adaptation of the flood story in the Epic of Gilgamesh, which predates Genesis by many centuries). Again, at the start of the Augustan age in Rome (after 31 BCE), Virgil in his Aeneid (twelve chapters, perhaps never completed) turned Homer's *Iliad* and *Odyssey* upside down (*Odyssey* first, in the journey narrative; *Iliad* last, in the war story on the Italian peninsula). While doing this, Virgil attributed divine origins to Rome's new tyrant, Octavian (Augustus) by means of a mythic Iulus, ancestor of Caesar's Julian clan. Eclesiastes 1:9 has it right: "There is nothing new under the sun."

Back to the Sator Square specifically:

Quick note on nomenclature: I suggest there was an ancient Roman farmers' saying, a Sator aphorism; which was then harnessed by a clever, literate oligarch in the big city, who devised the fiendishly clever and beautiful four-way palindrome through which the original aphorism or saying or proverb has come down to us in modern times.

Aside from the enduring sanctity of Neolithic cosmologies based on the annual crop cycle tied to the lunar and other life cycles, I am struck by an even deeper potential for visualization in the Sator aphorism. Namely, plowing is not just a metaphor for living our daily life and making decisions. Plowing implies sowing. Recall the Christian Testament Epistle to the Galatians (6:7), which reads: "As you sow, so shall you reap." The idea of sowing actions based on conscious decisions, and then reaping consequences, has thus been embedded in the human cultural idiom for thousands of years.

Upon deeper reflection, I see an even more profound connection with human history from the Neolithic revolution forward. The metaphor or metonym of plowing goes far deeper than the notion of driving a car, which I have offered as a way of bringing the notion of actions and consequences from the ancient Sator aphorism forward.

The language of the aphorism is metaphor, expressed as we see it.

The meaning, however, can be taken further as something like:

The begetter planted the seed of your life (or fate), but you are the seed-planter of your own fate in this world.

In that sense, the act of plowing (*opera*) becomes planting (same broad sense of 'farm work').

One must assume, finally, that the author of the Epistle to the Galatians must have been quite familiar with the Sator proverb, amid the general connectedness of ancient Mediterranean cultures and languages. What you shall sow, you shall reap. There is nothing new under the sun.

Bibliography & Further Reading

(Selected General Bibliography in My Library)

Adkins, Leslie and Roy: *Handbook to Life in Ancient Rome* (Oxford University Press, Oxford, 1998).

Allen, Richard Hinckley: *Star Names: Their Lore and Meaning* (G.E. Stechert, 1899; reissued in the U.K. by Constable & Co., Ltd; reissued in the U.S. by Dover Publications, New York, 1963).

Armstrong, Karen: *A Short History of Myth* (Canongate, Edinburgh, 2006).

Ashby see Platner.

Bauer, Susan Wise The History of the Ancient World From the Earliest Accounts to the Fall of Rome, W.W. Norton, New York NY 2007

Burris, Eli E. Burriss and Casson, Lionel: *Latin and Greek in Current Use* (Prentice-Hall, Inc., Englewood Cliffs, New Jersey)

Cassell: See Simpson.

Casson, Lionel: see Burris.

Childe, V. Gordon: *The Aryans* (Dorset Press, New York, 1987).

Claridge, Amanda *Rome* (travel guide) *Oxford Archeological Guides* OUP New York NY and London UK 2007 ISBN 0192880039

Cullen, John T. *The God Page: Learning From Three Historical Religious Modalities: Animist, Polytheist, Monotheist* (Clocktower Books, San Diego, Amazon, Kindle Direct Publishing (KDP) e-book ASIN B01F8FP3HQ rev. 2018).

Fishwick, Duncan: *An Early Christian Cryptogram?* (Canadian Catholic Historical Association, Toronto, 1959) ref. online by St. Paul's College, University of Manitoba: http://www.umanitoba.ca/colleges/st_pauls/ccha/Back%20Issues/CCHA1959/Fishwick.htm

Jobes, Gertrude and James *Outer Space: Myths, Name Meanings, Calendars, From the Emergence of History to the Present Day* (New York and London: The Scarecrow Press, Inc. 1964) with Foreword by Phillip D. Stern, F.R.A.S., Planetarium Director, Museum of Art, Science, and Industry at Bridgeport, Connecticut.

Koebler, Gerhard: *Neuhochdeutsch-indogermanisches Woerterbuch, 3e Auflage* (http://www.koeblergerhard.de/idgwbhin.html).

Lanciani, Rodolfo Amadeo (1845-1929) *The Ruins And Excavations of Ancient Rome* and other texts;e.g. *Pagan and Christian Rome* (1893) online (see Wikipedia bibliography at author name entry).

Pagliari, Federica: *Un Grande Enigma Che Attraversa Intatto I Millenni* (http://www.humnet.unipi.it/ital/cd2007/materiali/magiademo/testi _documentiMate/sator.htm)

Palmer, L.R.: *The Latin Language* (Faber and Faber, London, 1968).

Platner, Samuel B. and Ashby, Thomas *A Topographical Dictionary of Ancient Rome* (Cambridge University Press, Cambridge UK 2015 ISBN 9781108083249

Pokorny, Julius: *Indogermanisches Etymologisches Wörterbuch* (*Indo-Germanic Etymological Dictionary*, Bern: Francke, 1959, reprinted in 1989); ref. online by the University of Texas: http://www.utexas.edu/cola/centers/lrc/ielex/PokornyMaster-X.html).

Richardson, L. Jr. *A New Topographical Dictionary of Ancient Rome* (Johns Hopkins University Press, Baltimore and London, 1992).

Sheldon, Rose Mary: *The Sator Rebus: An Unsolved Cryptogram?* (*Cryptologia*, July 2003, U.S. Military Academy, West Point, New York, ref. online at http://findarticles.com/p/articles/mi_qa3926/is_200307/ai_n9291635/pg_1.

Sheldon, Rose Mary: *Espionage in the Ancient World: An Annotated Bibliography of Books and Articles in Western Languages* (McFarland, Jefferson, North Carolina, 2008) ISBN 978-0786437689.

Simpson, D.P.: *Cassell's Latin Dictionary* (MacMillan, New York: Fifth Edition 1968).

Smith,William: *A Dictionary of Greek and Roman Antiquities* (John Murray, London, 1875). Online:

Virgil, *Georgics iv.58* (http://classics.mit.edu/Virgil/georgics.html).

Watkins, Calvert: *The American Heritage Dictionary of Indo-European Roots* (New York, Houghton-Mifflin Company, 2000).

I offer these titles as part of my general reading and research on many topics in Roman history, topology, and more. Note: I know of no examplar of the Satorformel in the ancient city of Rome itself, which seems accidental, but presents a small puzzle in itself. If found all over the empire, why not in the imperial capital? Archeological work continues in Rome; no telling what discoveries may yet appear.